WRITTEN BY ROB ARCHANGEL
OWNER & CO-FOUNDER OF ARCHANGEL INK

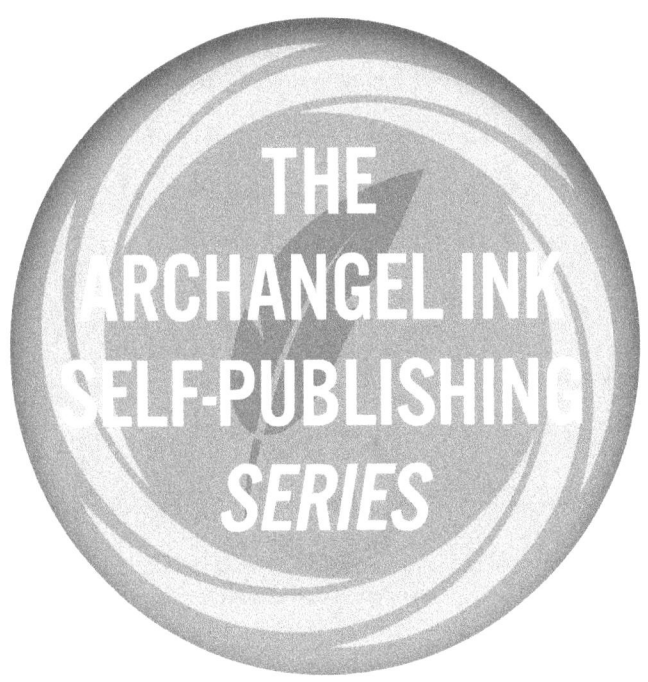

WWW.ARCHANGELINK.COM

Published by

www.ArchangelInk.com

ISBN-13: 978-1-942761-86-0

CONTENTS

INTRODUCTORY NOTE

Dear readers,

Thanks for picking up this short book. It is designed to help orient self-publishing authors to the industry, provide free and low-cost resources for the aspiring self-pubisher to get started, and give insight into what our company Archangel Ink can do to help authors, business professionals and entrepreneurs.

The content is adapted from our free series available at Archangelink.com. Please feel free to sign up and access this compilation there if you prefer. Each chapter is delivered via email once daily, and the introductory email also includes links to EPUB, MOBI and PDF formats available for immediate download.

Thanks again for reading, and we wish you the best in your self-publishing journey!

Rob Archangel

www.ArchangelInk.com

PART I

YOU JUST GOT *THIS* MUCH
CLOSER TO HAVING YOUR
OWN BOOK PUBLISHED

"Times are bad. Children no longer obey their parents, and everyone is writing a book."

– Marcus Tullius Cicero, 106-43 B.C

Rob Archangel here…

I'm glad you're reading this—right here, right now.

Why? Because EVERYONE *wants* to be an author. In fact, some polls show 9 out of 10 Americans want to write a book.

But you're different. Not only are you thinking about publishing your book, you're doing something most people will never do. You're taking action and getting the information you need to move forward with your dream of authorship. That's pretty cool.

At Archangel Ink, we've helped scores of authors experience what most people only dream about—writing and publishing their own book. We'd like to help you do the same if we're a good fit to work together.

That's why we've created this mini-course on publishing, kind of like painting a trail through a maze so you can envision the path from here to there.

"Here" is where you are now. You've gained some knowledge and wisdom to share with the world. Maybe you've become an expert in your field and want to write a book so you'll literally be the one who "wrote the book" on your topic. Maybe you've caught a vision for the residual income possibilities authors enjoy. Maybe you've got a message that's practically burning inside you, demanding to come out and reach people you can inspire to change the world—or at least a small corner of it.

"There" is where you want to go. It's the moment you're holding your own book in your hands, and your book is "out there" doing what you dreamed it would do.

Of course, from "here" to "there" is the maze.

Writing and publishing a book can be quite complicated.

And if you go the route of traditional publishing, it can be a road that's paved with rejection, heartache, and headaches.

So, by getting this little series we've created, you've made at least two really smart moves. One, you're taking action. Two, you're gaining a higher-level understanding of what goes into publishing your own book.

Here's what we'll cover:

- A couple of different ways you can go about getting your book written (without going crazy in the process).

- What happens after the writing phase is complete. Writing your book is only a small part of the publishing process… there's a lot more that has to happen.

- How to determine whether writing and publishing your book with Archangel Ink makes financial sense for you, or whether you'd be better off taking an alternate route to authorship (we'll show you that path, too).

- The part of publishing that most authors miss—marketing. There's no point in publishing your book if nobody's going to read it!

- What it's like partnering with Archangel Ink to move your book from an idea to the book shelf (or maybe you've got a manuscript in-hand already—that'll work, too!).

Once you've read through these next few chapters, you'll have a pretty clear understanding of what lies ahead for you. And if you decide to move forward with your book project, you'll get a feel for whether we are a good fit for you. That's important! You'll also understand a lot more about the process of writing and publishing a successful book, and you'll probably be even more excited about this possibility after you hear our take on what's possible for today's authors.

Also, if you decide that you'd like to work with Archangel Ink, you'll be several steps ahead of most authors because you'll have a deeper understanding about the process.

Knowing where you're going is always better than fumbling in the dark, right?

So, keep reading to learn more.

Until next time,

Rob

P.S. As you read through this brief six-part series, you may have some questions about your particular project. Just keep a list going! Most likely, we'll cover them in this mini course, but if not, or if you decide you're ready to take the next step, we'll schedule a complimentary call together. Sound good?

PART II

SO, CAN YOU REALLY
WRITE A BOOK?

"There is nothing to writing. All you do is sit down at a typewriter and bleed."

– Ernest Hemingway

Rob Archangel here…

Thanks, Ernest. That's great. Very encouraging.

Do you have your book written yet?

If you do, fantastic. You survived. You poured the information and inspiration that was in your brain out onto a screen, and you're ready for the next step toward publishing.

If not, even better! You can avoid what so many people consider to be an exhausting and painful process. More on that in a moment.

First, let's have a little chat about using your time wisely.

See, normally, you're busy doing your thing, whatever that thing is. You're coaching, consulting, selling, building businesses, teaching people... basically, doing the thing you're uniquely gifted to do. Great!

That's also why you're looking for information on publishing with Archangel Ink. Whether you've got a manuscript in hand or just a rough idea for your book, you know that writing is just a small part of getting your book into print. You know it's about to get even more time-consuming. There's learning how to do all the steps involved ... and then actually doing them. Unless your primary occupation is author, messing around with your book is probably not the most profitable (or enjoyable) way you could use your time. You do what you do—and we do this.

Whether we help you write your book or you hand off your manuscript and we run with it to to the finish line, one of the smartest moves you can make is partnering with an expert who's done it before.

So, let's say you have an idea for a book, but...

- You don't have time to write it. Ha! You don't have time for ANYTHING extra.

- You HATE writing. It gives you flashbacks of that mean teacher you had in middle school.

- You've had this idea for WAY longer than you'd like to admit, and even with the best of intentions, the book is just not happening. You're tired of just sitting there staring at a blank screen.

See? We've worked with many clients who've been right where you are. If the idea of writing your book seems overwhelming, we can help.

Can we share a little secret from the world of publishing?

MANY authors didn't write their own books. It's more common to partner with a ghostwriter than you'd imagine. It actually makes sense. Here's why:

You've got an idea. You're probably an expert in your field. (That's one great reason to publish a book, by the way— to reinforce your credibility and expert status.) You could probably talk about your topic for hours without breaking a sweat. It's so much a part of you that talking about it just flows effortlessly.

A good ghostwriter can help extract that expertise from you and get it into written form. (Don't worry, it doesn't even hurt.) What comes naturally to you is your message… what comes naturally to a ghostwriter is communicating that message—in YOUR voice.

Back in the "old days," using a ghostwriter was kind of a hush-hush deal. There was this sense that if you didn't physically put the words to the paper, you didn't write the book. It's not like that anymore! Now, it's all about collaboration.

You do what you do really well. What ghostwriters do really well is tell your story… and really good ones can do it so well that even your best friend won't guess you didn't actually sit down and write your book.

With Archangel Ink, there are a couple of ways we can help you get your book written:

1. You can give us an outline and we'll turn a ghostwriter loose on your topic. You tell the ghostwriter the key points you want him or her to emphasize, things to avoid, and perhaps a few resources to draw from, and the ghostwriter gets to work. Back and forth is minimal, and in exchange you get a great manuscript with relatively low cost. The writer will research, write, and deliver your completed manuscript. Voila! The writing part is done. Typically, this option runs about $1,000–$3,000 for a book that's about twelve to eighteen thousand words.

2. We can match you up with one of our custom ghost-writers. You'll provide an outline for your book, then go through a series of recorded interviews so you can just talk your way through the book's content. The writer will capture your thoughts, your expertise, your way of speaking, and put it all into writing. This is a much more collaborative process and generally takes longer, but the end result is fully vetted by and customized for the client. This custom option, of course, costs more, and is best for thought leaders who have unique and

specialized information and perspectives to share. You're looking at anywhere from \$2,500–\$25,000, depending on the particulars of your project and the experience of the writer you choose.

There's a third option, too. Some of our clients really want to write their own books, but could use some help in the form of an accountability partner, someone to hold their feet to the fire to keep them moving forward. This involves regular calls to discuss progress and troubleshoot issues as they come up. If you're in the midst of the writing process and know you need some outside help to get over the hump, we may be able to help. Reach out to us and we can discuss options for this sort of coaching.

In the end, writing your book can be pretty easy… even if you never pick up a pen (er… keyboard) yourself.

Give these options some thought if you don't already have your book written (or think about how much easier this route would be for the next one you publish).

Next up, we'll talk about what happens after the book is written… because there's a LOT more to do.

Until next time,

Rob

PART III

HERE'S YOUR SNEAK PEEK
INTO THE BLACK BOX
OF PUBLISHING

*"Everything should be made as simple
as possible, but not simpler."*

– Albert Einstein

Rob Archangel here…

There's a funny saying that goes something like this: The first 90% of publishing is writing your book. The second 90% is what comes after.

The math might be terrible, but the sentiment is right on target.

Publishing is a lot like a black box filled with mystery and tedium. Nice box, right?

The publishing world has a language all its own, debates that rage among experts, and more options than you might ever have considered.

The traditional publishing route is to find an agent who pitches your book to publishers, possibly gets a deal for you, and then you go on your merry way pouring your words out for their profit (maybe). We're a self-publishing business, so, no surprise, we're not huge fans of that route to authorship.

There's an easier way—and you're finding out about it now. We'll talk more about the differences between self-publishing and traditional publishing next time, but for the moment, let's dig into some options you have today that didn't exist before the Internet.

There are a few ways you can publish, and these options are quite meaningful because you can reach more people now than ever before AND earn money from your book at the same time. Here are the three primary ways you can publish. You can do one, some, or all:

- **Print your book.** We use—and recommend—KDP Print, which is owned by Amazon.com. It's a print-on-demand company, which means you NEVER have to have a garage full of books. You can buy one copy, a million copies, whatever you want. Your book will be available on Amazon for people to buy, and they mail it out, not you. You'll earn the difference between the printing costs and the price you set for your book.

- **Publish digitally on Kindle.** Again, Kindle is owned by Amazon. Your readers can read on a Kindle, an iPad, tablet, or another device like a laptop or desktop. You'll make either 35% or 70% of your book's list price, depending on a few factors.

- **Publish as an audiobook.** Guess who owns Audible. com, the world's biggest marketplace for audio books? Yes, Amazon. With professional narration and production, you can reach the crowd of people who'd prefer to listen than read. (Actually, if you want to do it yourself, you can do that, too. Here's a short eBook we put together offering a peek behind the veil of how and why we got started and the process we've used. Download at Archangelink.com/audible for free or learn more in our colleague Derek Doepker's *Audiobooks Made Easy Course*, available at Archangelink.com/Derek.)

Exciting, right?

Before you get too excited, though, we need to talk about editing. If you've written your own book, you're going to need a fresh pair of eyes (or more) to look it over and catch mistakes you can't see anymore because you're too close to the project.

There are several different tiers of editing we offer, outlined here: Archangelink.com/editing. Here's a short overview:

- **Developmental Editing:** This is high-level editing for the author who perhaps writes in "brain dump" fashion, putting all their thoughts down first and worrying about making it orderly and sequential later. The goal here is to make sure the material is laid out in a way that avoids repetition, has a consistent tone, doesn't leave anything vital out, and avoids repetition.

- **Manuscript Review:** A manuscript review provides great general feedback without the depth of a developmental edit. It's a good option if you're looking for feedback after a first draft to help identify your manuscript's strengths and weaknesses before beginning a rewrite.

- **Line Editing:** This is about the craft of writing. Is the language smooth and elegant? Can we rephrase a confusing sentence for increased clarity? Would a different word choice enhance the reader experience? Line editing involves multiple passes of review by the editor, and approval by the author. The goal is to present the author's thoughts in the most compelling and authentic way.

- **Line Edit Plus:** A combination of line editing and copyediting (details below).

- **Copyediting:** This editing focuses on the details: typos, grammar, consistency, and basic comprehensibility. Sentences that are inelegant but technically correct would be left intact.

- **Proofreading:** Proofreading overlaps with copyediting in that it focuses on irrefutable errors of grammar and spelling, while leaving anything else alone.

Proofreading is typically done on the final formatted draft, just before publishing. The proofreader will also look out for formatting structure and consistency (numbered lists, bullet points, header and sub header styling, etc. to ensure nothing was missed).

Just a few more nuts and bolts in the black box for today. Once your book has been edited, it needs to be formatted. You can't just upload an unformatted Word document and publish it as a book. There are a few types of formatting. Here's the breakdown:

- **eBook Formatting:** One of the advantages of eBook formatting is how straghtforward it is. These days, we primarily use Adobe InDesign for our clients, but not everyone has access to that application. For the DIYer, you can use MS Word and upload the file directly to Amazon, Lulu, or elsewhere. Send it through their in-house conversion process, and it will come out the other side as a file suitable for an eReader device, such as a Kindle, a Barnes and Noble Nook, etc. Bear in mind, there are lots of details to formatting and you need to know the basic rules involved to produce something that will look sharp and professional and won't have any distracting errors.

We've produced a skeleton file that you can download and write your manuscript in. This will do the basic formatting for you right out of the gate. You can find that at Archangelink.com/skeleton.

You can also go to a great free resource, The Smashwords Style Guide at Archangelink.com/smashwords. It's long and you'll want to take your time going through it, but it offers a great step-by-step guide to the practice and principles behind eBook formatting.

- **Paperback Formatting**: Print layout can be as simple or as complicated as you'd like to make it. Like eBook formatting, our team primarily uses Adobe InDesign these days, but we produced dozens and dozens of books using MS Word when we got started. One key thing to remember is that paperback formatting is fixed, meaning that the way it looks on screen is what it will look like on the page.

In contrast, eBook formatting is "re-flowable," meaning that the text will "flow" differently depending on the settings of the reader's device. Reader one might have Times New Roman, 10-point font with small margins and single spaces. Reader two might have Arial, 36-point font in purple, with huge margins, double spaces, and only 40 words per page. The unique formatting parameters of eBooks should allow for that customization.

If you'd like to create your own paperback edition, there are interior templates (Archangelink.com/CSinterior) and cover templates (Archangelink.com/CScover) that you can utilize to format your manuscript in a way that will look strong and professional. If you have special needs, you'll need to know more about the formatting parameters to tweak things so that they work for both your goals and meet technical standards. As of this writing, KDP Print ONLY does paperback publishing—it's far more economical than hardcover book publishing, and is what we recommend.

For more on both print and digital formatting, including demonstration videos, you can visit our blog post on the topic HERE: Archangelink.com/ book-formatting-can-i-really-do-it-myself-or-should-i-hire-a-professional.

Is your mind buzzing a bit? The possibilities ARE pretty exciting. Just think about how many people you can reach, how many readers might find your work, and the possibilities once your book gets OUT there.

Next up, we'll take a look at the whole publisher vs. self-publishing debate and what you need to think about money-wise as you move forward with your project.

Until then,

Rob

P.S. Yes, the process of getting your book ready for publication is complex, tedious, and far less sexy than you might imagine, but must be done. And honestly, we've done it so many times for really cool authors that we actually like it. Crazy, huh?

PART IV

WHAT'S THE BOTTOM LINE WHEN IT COMES TO PUBLISHING YOUR BOOK?

*"Nothing stinks like a pile of
unpublished writing."*

– Sylvia Plath

Rob Archangel here…

Hopefully, your head's not spinning from all the editing,
formatting, and publishing options we talked about last
time.

Once self-publishing opened up as an option, and aspiring
authors were no longer at the mercy of the big publishing
houses, there was instantly a LOT more to understand and
handle (if you're doing it on your own). The mainstream
publishers kind of poo-poo the self-publishing world, but
the explosion of new books is proof that people WANT to
get their message out there and will do what it takes to make
it happen.

Here's a quick-ish explanation of the state of publishing today.

Traditional publishing is tough for almost everyone. The likelihood that any author out there will be picked up by a publishing house is rather slim, and even if you land a publishing deal, it may not be as lucrative as you'd hoped.

Years ago, I tried to get a project picked up by a traditional publishing house and learned a bit about the process. You have to find an agent, write a book proposal or query letter, mail printouts of your manuscript (or excerpts of it) to the publishing house (typically via snail mail), and hope that the right person with the right frame of mind who's not hangry because they forgot breakfast that morning gets to it and gives it the green light to the next step.

Even if you get past the gatekeepers, traditional publishers still expect you to bring your own platform (followership) and do the legwork of marketing it and selling copies. They simply don't have bottomless pockets to shower every book in their stable with the love and attention it may need to reach its potential. If they offer you an advance and your book underperforms, you're on the hook for the advance payment they didn't recoup. For all this shared risk you assume as the author, large New York publishers typically offer an anemic 5–15% royalty on each copy of your book.

Self-publishing offers more-promising options. If you're going to be responsible for the legwork of selling your book anyway, maybe it makes sense to cut out the publishing house altogether and earn 35–80%+ of the sales price on each copy sold. For a paperback retailing at $19.99, for example, you might only earn a couple bucks with a big publisher, versus $10 or $15 per self-published copy.

That means you could sell five to ten times as many copies through a publishing house as on your own and still bring in a smaller paycheck. The difference in sales for self-published vs. traditionally published may not be dramatic enough to justify the lost percentage.

Self-publishing also has a much lower barrier to entry. You can price your book lower than the big guys, making you more attractive to new readers, yet still earn more per unit sold. Alternately, you can keep the price point comparable and earn substantially more per unit sold.

Self-publishing is a no brainer then, right? Yes and no.

The biggest advantage of traditional publishers is the ease they offer. You might be the best writer in the world, but that doesn't always translate to self-publishing success. You need to become competent at manuscript editing and proofreading, cover design, eBook formatting, paperback layout and design, audiobook narration, editing and mastering, and uploading your material to your chosen distribution channels. And that's not to mention sales copy writing, keyword and category selection, launch strategy and promotion, and ongoing marketing efforts.

You absolutely can do it yourself, but you may need some help and guidance along the way. That's where we come in. More on that later.

So, can you really make money writing and publishing books?

Many authors only think about royalty payments when

it comes to evaluating the earnings side of writing and publishing. You sell books, you earn income from those sales.

But that's NOT the only reason people write and self-publish. Sure, there are intangible benefits like the pleasure of telling a story, the joy of knowing your fans are hanging on your every word, or the fact you're leaving behind a legacy… in print.

There's another strategic reason many of our authors write and self-publish their books. Your book can serve as a powerful lead-generation tool. It's a great way to build your professional credibility and acclaim.

Let's say your ideal customer goes online looking for a solution you provide—or they go online to research before hiring you. They find your book, buy it, and next thing you know, they hire you.

Or, let's say you've got a hot prospect. You send a copy of your book (hint: you can even send one direct from Amazon and bypass the gatekeeper, virtually guaranteeing your prospect opens your package). Your prospect is impressed, understands that you're legit, and decides to hire you.

Under either of these scenarios, you don't care at ALL about royalties. You make your investment back through an increase in your business.

(I recently wrote a whole book on this topic, entitled *The Published Professional: How Self-Publishing Can Help Build Your Brand, Attract More Clients, And Increase Sales.* Available for free at Archangelink.com/TPP)

What does it cost to publish with Archangel Ink?

Honestly, we can't pin down a number. There are so many variables here, and the best way to get pricing for your particular project is to have a conversation with us. We'll tell you how to arrange that conversation in a later chapter.

To give you an idea though, you can see our current package pricing at Archangelink.com/packages

Until we chat, we encourage you to make a list of questions and pull together an idea of what you want to accomplish with your book. Are you aiming for a best seller that'll pay royalties? Or are you more interested in a book that leads your readers to take further action (like hiring you)? Having a plan for the financial end is the best way to ensure it makes sense for you to publish with us.

Next time,

Rob

PART V

DON'T IGNORE THIS PHASE IN PUBLISHING YOUR BOOK... A MISTAKE MOST AUTHORS MAKE

"Don't judge a book by its cover."

– Folk Wisdom… and baloney

Rob Archangel here…

If a tree falls in the forest, does it make a sound? Or, if an author publishes a book and fails to market it successfully, does it accomplish anything?

It would be fantastic if great books naturally created their own following, attracted the attention of ideal readers, and made a mint for their authors… all on their own.

But, yeah, that's a fantasy.

Trust me. If you hit "Publish" and nobody notices, it's a major disappointment.

When you self-publish, you're also responsible for promoting your book. (The funny thing is, even if you go with a traditional publishing house, you do the lion's share of promotion!) But that doesn't mean you've got to go it alone or feel your way in the dark.

Yes, they will judge.

The first and very BEST ad you can make for your book is the one most authors screw up the worst: the cover. You can't slap words and any old image on a cover and call it good. You certainly can't buy a cover on Fiverr and bank on it to do your book sales any favors. Today's readers are discerning and any hint of amateur quality discounts you immediately, leaving you in a fight to regain lost credibility out of the gate.

There's no avoiding it, no shortcut, and no substitute… Your cover MUST sell your book. That means it's got to fit in your genre, feature high-quality imagery or typeface/layout, and have a design that practically forces prospective readers to click on it.

Archangel Ink has some of the most compelling book

cover designs out there, and if we work together, you'll be astonished at what we can create together.

However, if you're leaning toward more of a DIY publishing experience, we don't want to leave you hanging and helpless! You can get an overview of the practice and principles of cover design, along with the requisite self-publishing skills in Dale L. Robert's DIY Publishing course Archangelink.com/Dale. Dale is a trusted friend of Archangel Ink, and great resource.

Beyond the cover…

We can't take over the promotion for you—it's kind of a never-ending task, after all. But we can help give you a major leg up as you ride this beast… actually a couple of legs up.

When it comes to book promotion, we continually survey the landscape to see what's working well, then we tweak our strategy to play the game the smart way. There are a couple of ways you can harness the power of our scouting.

First, you can check out *Book Launch Gladiator: The 4 Phase Approach to Kindle Book Marketing Success in 2018*, written by our own in-house Marketing Chair, Jordan Ring. It provides a highly-actionable overview on launching and promoting your book effectively as a first-time author, and is available **free** at Archangelink.com/gladiator

Second, because the whole of publishing success boils down to acting on a smart strategy, we give you access to marketing strategies we **KNOW** work well. Jordan offers a full course on the book launch including:

- How to choose the right keywords for your book so eager readers can find it on Amazon.

- Which categories you should choose—and which to avoid.

- How to write a killer book description.

- How to nab excellent, honest book reviews that will wow Amazon and your potential readers. (There are a LOT of fatal pitfalls you can avoid by knowing how to get reviews the right way.)

If you decide to go solo on creating and publishing your

book, you can also purchase the Book Launch Gladiator course at: Archangelink.com/BLG

The tactics you'll learn will help you stand out from the crowd and turn what could feel like a crapshoot into a coherent step-by-step process you can follow now, and for every book you write going forward.

In the end, successful publishing is largely dependent on marketing. You could have the most awesome book ever written, edited to perfection, formatted like a work of art, but if it falls on deaf ears, you'll end up with nothing but a broken heart (well, and maybe a broken bank account, too).

The Archangel Ink team wants to help you set yourself up to achieve your goals. In the next chapter, we'll talk a bit more about what it's like partnering with us on your book.

To your success,

Rob

PART VI

ARE YOU READY TO TAKE THE NEXT STEP TOWARD PUBLISHING YOUR BOOK?

"There is no greater agony than bearing an untold story inside you."

– Maya Angelou

Rob Archangel here…

Now that you've learned so much about self-publishing, hopefully it's starting to feel real.

If you haven't run for the hills screaming, you're probably more serious than ever about writing and publishing your book.

Now it's time to look a little more at what's involved in working with Archangel Ink.

First… a little "unselling"

We're not cheap. We're professionals at what we do, and that means we do it right. We know that we're not going to be a good fit for everyone. Our services are labor intensive and high value, and our practices are based on years of experience—we know what works well and what doesn't.

Clients who work with us do so because they trust us and want to hand over the reins to make the best decisions for them that we can. For authors who want a more self-directed experience with a lot more control over the many details involved, we do offer a couple of options at a lower price point.

- **The first is the DIY Publishing Course** Archangelink.com/Dale It's several hours of video training providing a guided overview of the steps involved in putting a book together. It covers researching your niche, writing quality content, self-editing and proofreading your manuscript, formatting for eBook and paperback distribution, navigating distribution options, marketing strategy and more.

We used to offer an in-house Archangel Ink DIY Course, but Dale's is much better and more up-to-date. If you're trying to figure out if it's worthwhile to hire us or go at it yourself, this DIY course is a great first step. After you take it, you'll have a sense of whether or not the process is for you. If you are long on time and shorter on funds, as many authors starting out can be, this can be a great option for you.

- **The second option for authors looking for a more self-directed experience is a consultation with us.** We're happy to connect, listen, and provide some feedback to direct you along your way. This allows us to assist authors even if they don't work with us. It's an efficient way to help and allows us to avoid time-consuming email chains that pull us from our clients.

We offer one free 30-minute call. If you need further guidance, and the other resources we've directed you toward are not quite enough, we are happy to set up subsequent calls and answer questions for you. Our current rate is $200/hour, available in $50 (fifteen-minute) blocks. Sometimes it's just easier to spend a few minutes on the phone and have immediate feedback from an experienced professional; other times it's nice to have an accountability partner, someone to check in with on a rolling basis as you make your way through the self-publishing process. Whatever your needs are, we're here to help, and these consultations allow you to obtain precisely the level of help you need.

Now, if you DO think we'd make a good team for publishing your book, here's what to do:

Remember that complimentary 30-minute call I mentioned a moment ago? We're happy to connect with you and answer your questions. If you're looking to work with us on a full-service package, this is a good chance to feel us out and get a better sense of how we might help with your specific needs.

You can ask questions, request a proposal based on the details of your project, and find out more about the next steps.

ALL YOU HAVE TO DO TO SCHEDULE YOUR COMPLIMENTARY SKYPE CALL IS EMAIL REPLY@ARCHANGELINK.COM

We'll take it from there and find a time that works for everyone's schedule.

Thanks for letting me pull back the curtain a bit on the whole writing and publishing process. It's an incredible honor and privilege to work with our authors and help them get their messages out to the world.

I hope this information has been helpful.

Best to you,

Rob Archangel

ABOUT THE AUTHOR

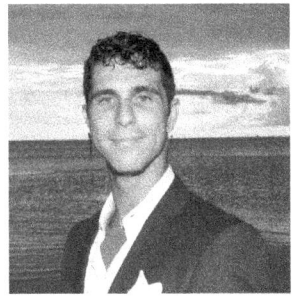

Rob Archangel is the owner of Archangel Ink, and author of *The Published Professional: How Self-Publishing Can Help Build Your Brand, Attract More Clients, And Increase Sales.* For several years, he worked as assistant to the publisher of the longest running permaculture journal in North America, and came to appreciate the power of the published word. In 2012, he entered into the world of digital ebooks, print-on-demand paperbacks, and audiobooks and hasn't looked back. Realizing a knack and a passion for the process, Rob founded Archangel Ink to help clients more effectively reach their audience, share their message and build their brand. Rob and his team help busy authors, entrepreneurs and business professionals self-publish their written work with quality and ease, so they can focus on their area of expertise.